The very first line of "In the City of Tenderness and Desperate Promises," the official opening poem in Aaron Coleman's evocative and blistering *Red Wilderness* is this: "Punctured in the soft hour, we tried a new way home . . ." That unproven path winds "all up in through here," past mudglut banks, trees ripped with ghosts, Red Lick and St. Louis, rain-pelted ruins and through America's slick and murderous landscape—and straight toward the tumult and testimony of Black days, both here and behind us. On the way to "home and never home," these keen and luminous poems chronicle what is ultimately a way for Black folks to thrive in the midst of storm.

PATRICIA SMITH

The ancestral song of Aaron Coleman rings true in *Red Wilderness*, clearing a way for us to see up ahead. There's the legacy of family and of the community we build outward, and then there's the wilderness, that country, around us all, which Coleman maps out, showing us "what is true but nameless," and that which "knows no beginning or end." Whether he offers a reverie from a crooner, "somewhere smiling, / as new friends glide together," or we fall into, "a black boy's body . . . a language sculpted out of silence," what's clear is that Coleman is a cartographer of our sensibilities, our fears, and our hopes for a space we can call our own.

A. VAN JORDAN

With linguistic precision and a tenderness that not only brings places, times, and people to life, but also demands that you, the reader, cares for them, Aaron Coleman offers us a massive achievement with *Red Wilderness*. Inventive, direct, and stunning in approach, its greatest achievement, to my eye, is the transportative nature of it. "A black boy's body is a language sculpted out of silence," Coleman writes, and you might, perhaps, know the boy, or know the body, or know the silence, or know all three. For this, more than anything, *Red Wilderness* is an incredibly generous offering. One that will echo through my world for years to come.

HANIF ABDURRAQIB

Red Wilderness is a map of stories and songs inseparable from their folks: soldiers, lovers, kin, citizens, ancestors—some pinned to history, some near-erased, others floating through holy or brutal scenes and memorials. Coleman voices these voices; he counts the countless instances of State violence against Blackness and Black futures. Whether from memory, history, or imagination, the voices in *Red Wilderness* speak here in iterations of love, resistance, wonder, connection, truth, and joy. Coleman's brilliant signature is his ability to voice many people, while keeping each individual's sound: a maestro directing an intergenerational community choir of soloists—an historical ensemble pulled from the dead and the living—in an epochal opera.

BRENDA SHAUGHNESSY

Red Wilderness

Red Wilderness

POEMS

AARON COLEMAN

FOUR WAY BOOKS

TRIBECA

LIBRARY OF CONGRESS CATALOGING-IN-PUBLICATION DATA
Names: Coleman, Aaron, author.
Title: Red wilderness / Aaron Coleman.
Description: New York : Four Way Books, 2025.
Identifiers: LCCN 2024035176 (print) | LCCN 2024035177 (ebook) | ISBN
   9781961897243 (trade paperback) | ISBN 9781961897250 (ebook)
Subjects: LCGFT: Poetry.
Classification: LCC PS3603.O4324 R43 2025 (print) | LCC PS3603.O4324
   (ebook) | DDC 811/.6--dc23/eng/20240816
LC record available at https://lccn.loc.gov/2024035176
LC ebook record available at https://lccn.loc.gov/2024035177

This book is manufactured in the United States of America and printed on acid-free paper.

Four Way Books is a not-for-profit literary press. We are grateful for the assistance
we receive from individual donors, public arts agencies, and private foundations
including the NEA, NEA Cares, Literary Arts Emergency Fund, and the
New York State Council on the Arts, a state agency.

We are a proud member of the Community of Literary Magazines and Presses.

Dedicated to my late uncle, Rick Ward,
and to all my family on both sides who've done so much genealogical work,
who've shared so many stories with me, wondering and weaving together our lives.

CONTENTS

2

". . . lit with red life, / the holler of survivor's blood . . ."

3

"Three levels underground I pushed upon a heavy metal door marked 'Danger' and descended . . ."

There are lessons to learn from those
who make homeland in wasteland, freedom routes to chart
that start in a ship's hull, debris of mad and black life
to retrieve from the sea, mad black worlds to make
that rise from a ship's wake, and questions that refuse answers but rouse movements.

~La Marr Jurelle Bruce *How to Go Mad without Losing Your Mind:*
Madness and Black Radical Creativity

Take a look at this map here. You see that right there?
That's a city. It's only a half a mile by half a mile . . .
but that's a city.—It's made of bones.

~Phylicia Rashad as Aunt Ester
in August Wilson's *Gem of the Ocean*

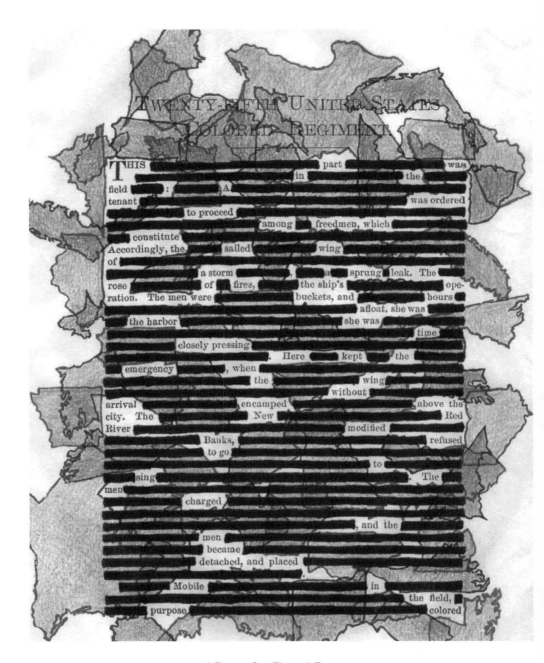

TWENTY-FIFTH UNITED STATES COLORED REGIMENT

THIS ▮▮▮▮▮▮ part ▮▮▮▮▮ was field ▮▮▮▮▮ in ▮▮▮▮▮ the ▮▮ : ▮▮▮▮ A ▮▮▮▮▮ tenant ▮▮▮▮▮▮ was ordered ▮▮▮▮▮ to proceed ▮▮▮▮▮ among ▮▮ freedmen, which ▮▮▮▮ constitute ▮▮▮▮ Accordingly, the ▮▮▮ sailed ▮▮▮ wing of ▮▮▮▮ a storm ▮▮▮▮ a ▮ sprung ▮ leak. The rose ▮▮ of ▮ fires, ▮▮ the ship's ▮▮▮ ope- ration. The men were ▮▮▮▮ buckets, and ▮▮▮ hours ▮▮▮ afloat, she was ▮▮ the harbor ▮▮▮▮ she was ▮▮▮ time ▮▮▮ closely pressing ▮▮▮▮. Here ▮▮ kept ▮ the ▮▮ emergency ▮▮ , when ▮▮▮ the ▮▮▮ wing ▮▮ without ▮▮ arrival ▮▮▮ encamped ▮▮▮ above the city. The ▮▮▮ New ▮▮▮ Red River ▮▮▮▮ modified ▮▮ Banks, ▮▮▮ refused to go ▮▮▮▮ to ▮▮ sing ▮▮▮▮ . The ▮▮ men ▮▮▮ charged ▮▮▮ , and the ▮▮▮ men became detached, and placed ▮▮▮ Mobile ▮▮▮ in ▮▮▮ the field, ▮ purpose ▮▮▮ colored

i. Figures One Through Two

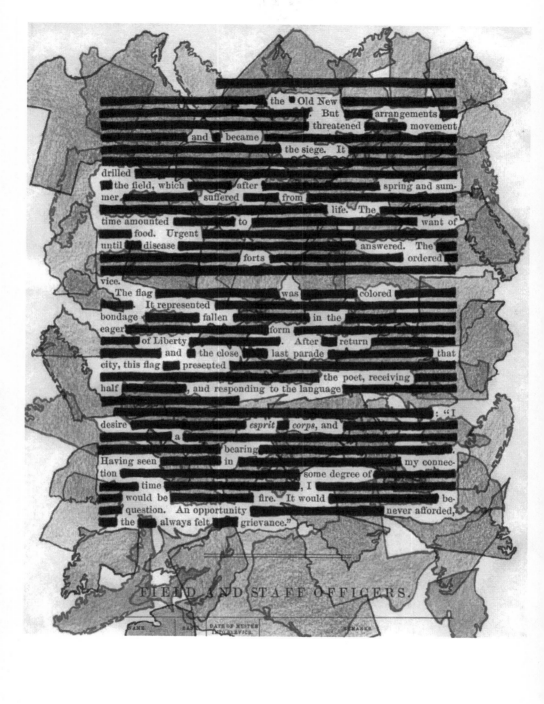

the ██ Old New
But ████ arrangements
threatened ████ movement
and ██ became
the siege. It
drilled ████████
████ the field, which ██████ after ████████ spring and sum-
mer ██████ suffered ████ from
████ life. The ████ want of
████ food. Urgent
until ██ disease ████████ answered. The
████ forts ████ ordered
vice.
The flag ████ was ████ colored ████
████ It represented ████
bondage ████ fallen ████ in the
eager ████ form
████ of Liberty ████. After ██ return
████ and ██ the close ██ last parade ████ that
city, this flag ██ presented
████ the poet, receiving
half ████, and responding to the language
████ : " I
desire ████ *esprit* *corps*, and
████ a
████ bearing
Having seen ██ in ████ my connec-
tion ████ some degree of
████ time ████, I
would be ████ fire. It would ████ be-
question. An opportunity ████ never afforded,
the ██ always felt ██ grievance."

FIELD AND STAFF OFFICERS.

1

Time and place have had their say.
ZORA NEALE HURSTON

In the City of Tenderness and Desperate Promises

Punctured in the soft hour, we tried a new way home
past the pawn shop neon-green with memory. She
came away with me from broken roads. Bird bone
litters tall, forgotten weeds. We paused to try to see

inside each fractured hollow. But hard rain hurried us
as slanted ground that was a risk became a gulch—
silent, tilted heads appeared to pray on a passing city bus,
but eyes lie—Who am I to say that I have seen too much

   to trust another stranger? To learn to start over?
   The end got here before us. Each footprint deep and flooded
   with chemical runoff; technicolor surfaces, but no real border.
   Bones don't float; the birds' or our own. The route turned

blue and bottomless, but it wasn't waves and isn't
water. Just consequence. We wander in wet endless sound
and learn to call it falling—until she says, "This love is a decision
not to forget, but to keep going." Nothing else. I wonder if we are bound

to drown in chance and mangled maps. Slick with rain, rock moss riots
money-green until tornado-green, churning, like our city's restless silence.

Another Strange Land: Downpour off Cape Hatteras (March, 1864)

For my ancestor
in the Pennsylvania 25th Colored Infantry
aboard the Suwanee

First a penny-sized hole in the hull
                        then eager saltwater rushing over
    us and clouds swirling and clotting
        the moonlight—no time to stop and look upon it
as the hole erupts into an iron mouth,
                screeching as it peels and tears
                        open iron as iron should not open—

muffled and heavy   us turning underwater
                        we confused the metal echo and thunder
        as the same death knell from God's mouth—

we been done   floated all this way down
            in dark blue used
        uniforms, how far from slavers' dried-out fields
in Virginia, Pennsylvania—wherever

                        we came from now we
        barely and only
                see and hear an ocean
                        whipped into storm

not horror, not glory, but storm
                not fear, not power, but focus
        on the work of breathing, living as the storm
rocks us and our insides upside down   turns
        hard tack into empty nausea—

so close to death I thought I saw the blaze-
sick fields of Berryville again, curling fingers
                    of tobacco, hurt fruit and flower—
but no, but   no.

I say no to death now. I'm nobody's slave
                        now. I'm alive   and not alone,
one of those   who escaped and made   myself
              a soldier a weapon a stone in David's sling
          riding the air above the deep. I grow more dangerous
to those who want me. I ain't going back
                        to anywhere I been before.

    I grab a bucket. You grab a bucket. We the 25th
Pennsylvania Colored Infantry, newly formed
                    and too alive and close to free
    to sink below this midnight water. 36 hours—chaos
shoveling-lifting-throwing   ocean back into ocean
                    to reach land and war in the Carolinas.

    I stole my body back   from death and going down
                more than once. I steal my breath
tonight and every night   I will not drown.

"I could always just hear somebody running"

~Fred Moten (in conversation with Saidiya Hartman on "The Black Outdoors")

Reeling here out past the woods where
somebody's running—listen, gone river the edge
where feet leaped slick

and swum faith so across it was
a choice a swimming in
ruse-ripped scent-lifted safe

locked tracked place
hold nevered breathed
in mudfish catfish gill-lit

fish maw heavy-heavy in air—rich stench so
moody sexing the water—light
might moon the current to

take you, touched terror,
safely across itself
a savoir for a second only

in a second second deadly—
becoming leeway
becoming a way from

what you hear, here, howling
animals—not hounds, not us—in sites
of no and could and always

splayed black gravity
       floating across remembering
pine needles and hard feet

       tree sap leak help me help
you reach past
       the sum of life split with its

death—together land gasps
       separates and bloodies
the night thrush sensorium the in

       being seethe, the wayward out
that fails the end, here
          hold on to me

I Found Kin in a Thrift Store Photograph

Above my bed a black boy leans
his chin down on the dark wood

of a small bridge, his arms
loose over the edge, far above

the rushing water. His fingers
let the wind's anonymous grace spill

through him. The night is cinders:
flecks of bluish white and human red

trapped inside the sky. His face so
swept up in shadow his expression is

full of the unknowable. A black boy's body
is a language sculpted out of silence.

Outside of time, inside the picture
this anonymous child has come

to be my family. Somehow
his legs sway with the framed waves

at the same pace loneliness slips
beneath the surface of intuition, floods

the warm current called desire.
On the far side I will never see

his spine is my creation myth, a bone river
of redemption, a choice to live, despite

unkeepable love. This religion of slow loss
balanced on the balls of his feet.

S t (r) a y (1860$\frac{1}{2}$3?

For my ancestor(s) who took South Mountain
from Virginia to Pennsylvania (and everywhere else),
for all who freed themselves and kept going

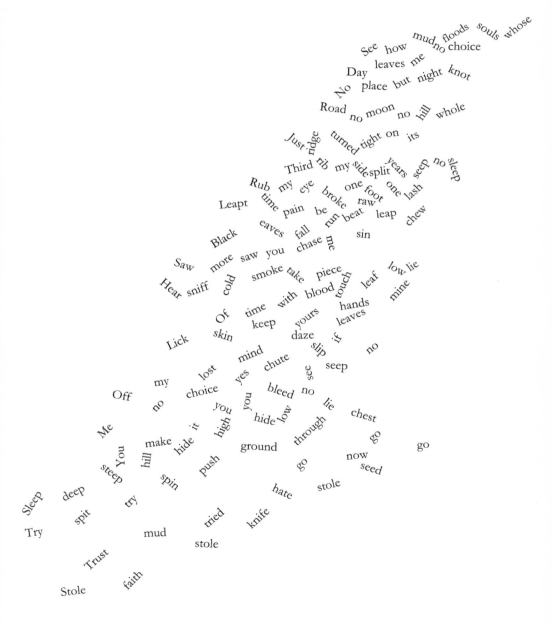

See how mud no choice floods souls whose
leaves me
Day
No place but night knot
Road no moon no hill whole
Just ridge turned tight on its
Third rib my side split years seep no sleep
Rub my eye broke one foot one lash
Leapt time pain be raw leap chew
Black eaves fall run beat sin
more saw you chase me
Saw cold smoke take piece low lie
Hear sniff leaf mine
Of time with blood touch hands
keep yours leaves
Lick skin daze slip if no
mind chute see seep
my lost yes bleed no
Off choice you lie chest
no you hide low through go go
Me make hide it high ground go now
hill push spin go seed
You steep hate stole
Sleep deep try
spit tried knife
Try mud stole
Trust
Stole faith

Of Walking In

I have taken the risk and liberty
of empathizing with the ill and braggadocious
brothas walking around Saint Louis

shout-singing their favorite pop hip-hop songs
in order to perform a riddle and posture
of freedom. I caught myself singing, too,

getting louder and louder as I walked
across another cavernous pandemic night. Past
questions of hope and hopelessness. I trudged. I made

up the song I sang as I went, trickling down
patterns and headlight shine, but I
know I felt the big black weightlessness

in the practice of letting go
of public fear and private shame
in public space. Untaken, but noticed.

The Forest's Edge (Summer, 1864)

*For my ancestor
inside Fort Pickens,
Pensacola Bay, Florida*

The stillness of the wood across the bay
is a lie. What blinded us
        when the orange moon opened

    the night the way
        sick bloat opened the gut
of my brother? Again, another one, my north

        light in the hard soot sky. This dark's
too full of heavy shells and shot and roofless
           rooms. Look up. No, don't trust

    fear more than pain. Pray we turn
the hurt into something free. If not
        now, then when—We tried

        to speak. They took
    his teeth. My eyes
        pick distances then keep

on roaming. I held his hand
        that night he passed. Felt cold fill
his palm, claim his arm, creep past the knot

        that was his elbow. His skin forgot
panhandle heat. I don't blame
        those that chose to leave

another place again, in

desertion or death, in

        dark or broad daylight. You run

    when you have to go. Sometimes I'm still

surprised by the strength of numb feet,

        the way the spine holds

    shoulders. Heard slavers

'cross the bay inside Barrancas got it bad

        too, death thickens the air, less

    from our guns than thirst and hunger.

What's war on a sinking island

        where men can't feel the ground?

     *

    The harbor grew

        hollow. I learned

the fungus in the gator's

          jawline, in the cypress

knees, black water, and

        broken teeth. We

strained the long way. We

         waited for our dead

    to end

the war for us. I learned

to read the blood
spills in dirt redder than red earth,
got lost
without leaving
our post. I pay
such close attention
now I almost love
the silences between
the living. Don't nobody
have to tell me
negroes raised these walls
around us years before
this war. Most
nights I listen close
enough to hear the breath
of black folk freeing
themselves, hiding
their way here, risking
everything I risked to
own their own bones, to
keep their blood. I tell them:
welcome, stay ready,
I don't know
when we'll go.

Promise

At the founding of Mount Tabor African Methodist Episcopal Church
ca. 1870, Mount Holly Springs, Pennsylvania

144 pine planks and logs and many thousand stones
palm-pressed into place, faith cladding

the cabin crevices and the woods
make an altar, birth tabernacle

roots I swear by the Lord's
Grace will take me home

"Oh you think you bad, huh?"

For my brotha, D

This crazy white boy Sam ran up on my giant goofy friend
and slammed his huge baseballer forearm against his temple,
against the side of my brotha's head as we stood together,
backs against our lockers. Caught us both by surprise
on some random morning in our early teenage years. My brotha
slid to the ground as the white boy stood right there, smiling—
so the moment swelled with silence
as too many fifteen-year-olds to count somehow all of a sudden
became quiet and watched as something primal
and American between black and white boys spilled out
of raucous what-if daydreams and confronted all of us with *oh shit*
and *what now* and none of us stopped to think *why* or *what for*? Even now
I remember the coarse iron feeling in my shoulder blades and a stone
contortion on my face, but I was still just standing there,
unmoving—was it even one breath later?—when my brotha slowly stood up
and said too calmly "oh you think you bad, huh?"
then snatched the crazy white boy by the collar and wailed on his face
with his meaty fist again and again as Sam's strong arms flailed
wildly trying to land somewhere as D backed him up then down the hall
while a sea of wide-eyed almost-children flowed around the two of them.
I struggled to keep up. The crazy white boy's nose opened: blood was everywhere
in his mouth on his clothes and spattered over D's sky blue polo
that was now ripped and all I could make myself do was watch
as they poured down the hallway. I don't remember the teachers or in-school police
officer breaking them up, I just remember D's solemn face through the window
glass as he sat in the main office afterwards, but I think I had his glasses
and I don't know where the crazy white boy went
but this other small and sort of friendly white kid came up to me
with enchantment on his face and adrenaline in his voice
and halfway whispered, "you're the king of the school now

since D beat up Sam and everybody knows you could fuck up D"
and I don't remember what I said to him
but I do remember my confusion. The feeling of being watched
in yet another way now and how D probably would have whooped my ass
or anybody else's as he rampaged in a straight line down that hallway
and how crazy-ass white boy Sam seemed so unpredictably dangerous—where was he
now?—I didn't feel like the king of anything, I felt forced into being
some new level of big black imposter. And sure, I was a monster
on the football field or in the paint on the basketball court or
with a smooth round metal shotput in my hand, but what kind of king did this
small naive white boy speak of? What was he so excited to see me lord over? What
was he wishing onto me, or into me? What kind of violence did he want more of?
I don't remember what happened next. I do remember, some months later
D's stepdad tried putting his hands on D, and the stepdad got knocked out, too.
A year or two later my brotha D got sent away
to some kind of "troubled youth" boot camp and suddenly
there were no more parental car rides together to the movies or mall
not to see or buy anything but just to walk around or sit down somewhere different
in our young bodies together, laughing and talking shit, mostly
minding our own business, but on the lookout, daring
anybody to start anything with us.

I Know It Was the Blood

There is no place in her Bible for "whereabouts unknown."
~ "The Idea of Ancestry" Etheridge Knight

Branches carry loss

through this red wilderness—

a pulse that bleeds across

the whole of us (say this is)

pierced long, then quick—

a life, never alone

American BirthDeath Sequence, 1919

They stole my baby out the jail
I never saw him again
until I saw him everywhere—
even all over your face
even in you

It took white gravel, her
        shout, his broken
wrist, midnight, and two
      cigarettes
            to be ready
                to witness
the world thrown in blue light.

Silence, hands, awareness, moons
      lifting my raw body
             then, my legs
falling

      out of the stone-muted room. Fear
stole flight. Cavernous absence the color of my mind's

blank sky. My spirit
      taut
on its hooked shadow, each cricket, each smattered

      blade of grass tilted past
wickedness, when
      touch turns into sickness—
           wind-frantic—

as frantic as the eyes
    (so many eyes)
                in competition for what

remains blood-colored,
      unsounded. Hidden

in a wood—

All up in through here

Best believe our people been living all up in through here
round these woods
for longer than anyone remember
I would say

way down back that way till the lip of the creek
and back East this way out
where the crops and trees change and air taste different
yes

what I do know now is you and my kin round here used to walk
all the way up into
those foothills there where the rocks full grown and the dirt stay dust
enough to rise and float

The Bright River We Keep

Outside Homer, Louisiana (1927)
For my Great Grandmother Harris

The broken rhythm of potholes and worn paint points us south
along the long road

we wanted and traced but feared to
speed down; sun-beamed and heavy as

an old-growth tree trunk uprooted floats
in loose parallels down

the bright river we keep
glimpsing behind aisles

of slender forest and ever-hills. Nowhere's our everywhere. Juniper
wood slices past us as we go. Shrewd and unabashed angles

take turns working the mud grass shore. I remind me to breathe. I don't
know when to touch you or myself

so I keep my hand
against my face—What does carefulness do to love?

Where are courage and loss taking
us, and do I have a choice? What's chasing

us—I know, I've known. A chance of sirens ambles over
the slow blue bend of this time, touches

horizon haze in front of us. Heat gambles
sweat down my spine as we cross

brittle railroad tracks. Getting farther, so getting closer.
Up ahead: the sign I didn't know

we needed clinks and hums. I hear and I believe
an old engine churning and rolling

its metal realm closer
and closer to us. Red dirt tests my lungs. I trust

the sunset light on the far side of my closed eyes. *Let me
go now, pull over. You can go.*

Surrender is a cold rain.

Prone red leaves—our veined backs bowing
to the end—   we lie down in bed, me next
                                                                                    to her, I teach my hand rest
                                    in her hand. She speaks
up into the ceiling, breathes   pearl blue
        winter   past and through   my palm, says:
                                                                there's an aperture where
                                                your fate line
                                                                        shudders, it looks
                                                like a wall
                                                                of falling water. I watch the angles
of a spider and whatever else
        crosses her night window: pause and climb, pause
and climb
                        Your heart   line leans
                                        long as the angle of a cave
                                closing itself in
                                        pitch blackness, a brightness
                                full of echoes.
                                                Who's praying   screaming
alone? I remain   attentive, calm—felled   moon and moonlight
    because I cannot   hear her.
    Distance holds   a forest in her eyes.
That's all I know.
                        Your head line is slicksweet,
                                        is the purple tentacle   of the octopus
                                        you ate in the heat
                        of a market   far from home.
                                Your fault line—What I am
drips and smears, the weight of want   shadows our bones. I watch her
    mouth, how it chooses   to move and not move.   My hand still

             in her hand, I watch her pain
slip open, become a clutch of tendrils

                              burrowed in my own. Touch happens when I stop
         wondering what a man and woman do   with power.

Deep Pleasure

I found a border in my body, slipped my fingers over
its simple seam until
I felt its stitches unwind and open. Out come scattered

brick walls, an autoworker's ruined shoulder, hard clay
burned the color of bloodshot eyes, glass

skyscraping sugarcane with syringe tips
like hypodermic needles, the powerful
tongues of my fathers and my mothers lit with dying

sallow leaves and the vicious wind that runs
through their hollow, viruses and languages on stilts teetering

toward their next source of warmth. What did not run
was the tin daguerreotype of a white man
I thought was ugly until I knew to love

the thick scar that swims along his throat. The photo's
throat. Its lampblack coat. That pulse of silence before

rough music. His fragile Adam's
apple my past, a knot, a frozen petal
on my tongue, what blood calls back

into the void that was the home. What I am:
seven generations of yes as the carnival tears

night out of morning. My fingers make a map. My eyes crawl
back across the treeflower of my chest and watch
its wilted seams move like lips

in unison. What I am swallows whole
the buzzard's beak, the culture's talons: say *no, no more, no.*

Collision Test Fool

My crash. So realistic: I don't want
anyone or anything to
                come back
        as is. Being alive lies
where façade cracks. My model mock-up body sits
knees to chin against this abandoned
                    crumbling imperial wall, world
        divider, whistling low this slow-
mixed dixie, creolific
        cacophony branded scream
             song—At six,
saw Kunta get whipped
        and internalized a problem
                with being possessed, since then
                I've belonged to rhythm.
            Probably before
to that species of mind
            silence, in collusion in collision
        at a busted American six-point intersection:
                yellow-red-green gone
wild as the murk pulling the myth
                of the Mississippi, which is the bones
        in the left hand of my home—Now
I'm the signal flagged, now
            I'm the vectors deep as the fever
river in the rearview. My makeshift spine
                absorbs and leaps the impact
        of each crash. I don't clench
or speak, just torque:
             lithe recycled muscle mixed-
with cheap metal, crushed.

ii. Battle Flag of the 25th United States Colored Troops:
"Strike for God and [...] 25th United States Colored Troops" (1863-1865)

Battle Flag: "Strike for God and [...] 25th United States Colored Troops" (1863–1865)

Is the lost word "Liberty?" Barefoot and open-palmed,
one musket between us, them. Between a goddess, Columbia, and
a person enslaved. Each with one hand holding

the wood and iron body of
the flintlock, pointing the muzzle and bayonet up
at the navel of some impossible sky

swept under arch arcing into a circle, a window, a vision reaching
down and around, clasped by leaves unknown to me, a single vine,
fugitive laurels adorn: this forest's edge, pedestal, proclamation,

gown, worn hand-me-downs, rippled printed sky, broken ankle
chains, faded banners, letters, faded whiteness, blackness. Why
would a deity make a slave, then free that slave

to be a soldier? I only see time—until I see *through* time.
One hundred and fifty-nine
years later in front of Philadelphia's

City Hall, brother Marcus with his lens and I
run into an elder, a Civil War reenactor, suited in blue with white gloves,
his mustache salt and pepper, angular shoulders, not quite smiling,

gripping the same deep blue flag in today's gray light. He says "When enemies
saw this here white woman and black man together on this flag
they'd lose their minds or at least be

distracted long enough to get killed." We look
at threads and hands, their eyes, the weapon, colors
billow and crack in the wind of another day.

iii. In front of Philadelphia City Hall and Harriet Tubman Statue (March, 2022)

American Football

I wanted to be a trophy before I wanted to be a man.
I wanted to be a weapon before I wanted to be safe.

My helmet is a mask. Pencil-thin bars
              cage my face, fiberglass and hard white pads

          hug my skull. I know the boy I am. I know
     the boy in the body of a man

          who wants to be precise violence.
A skilled threat on a torn field—

       our bodies decorate the coliseum ground.
            We reset and collide. We draw each line

where faith bangs against brutality, where
      pain headlongs into desire. I remember

               my ringing ears and trotting softly
      to the sideline called home

after I launched my body into a boy
          who cradles a ball and escapes

in zagging lines, side to side as if his life
          depends on it. *Get up off the ground.* I fear

         what I've done to my body—
my blood filled with the sound

      of mothers chanting battle cries
          over their rampant sons. The quiet brooding

fathers. Maybe I'll always be the boy trying to find the eyes
of a miraculous girl lolling in the stands, deep in her own game, looking away

from the cage over my face—
sprawled in my first autumn,

I learn the taste of my own sweat—
to be black and uniformed defines

my body as a sacrifice. I wanted to be a trophy
before I wanted to be a man. I wanted to be a weapon

before I wanted to be safe. I fear I'm still that brutal dream,
body strapped inside devotion—

I can't imagine my calloused hands relaxed
at my sides, tenderness left open.

2

. . . lit with red life, / the holler of survivor's blood . . .
ARACELIS GIRMAY, FROM "AFTER"

Ruin in the Era of Rain

Even this rain
settles on the graceless

                              crowds and leaves
                              everything slick and rotting

                    beneath cavernous clouds
                    toting thunder—but who

lives in this wind
lying and laying down

                    a thin film
                    of stone shine, of old shame

                              against which I see
                              what kind of rage

take people's faces? They are tormented
tormenting me. Contestants believing

                    in a rumorous ceaseless
                    ancient violence

I refuse in my breath
and in the soles of my feet—

I refuse in my marrow, my sorrow
and in the long shot of my bones—

Outside Homer, Louisiana

For my Great, Great Grandmother, Ma Shug

Hush now. Go deep:
deeper now
into the woods

where she
would build
her quiet

kingdom, her
summers swept in
north Louisiana heat.

Her descendants, my
elders. She taught them
the many languages of trees,

squirrels, shotguns, life
beyond the barrel
of any town, outside the limits

of most people. Ma Shug opened
her arms to
hold wide the childhood

south of my father,
uncle, aunt,
grandmom, granddad,

who was first her
grandson. My Ma Shug opened
all of them so also me to

her wilderness called love. Way
deep in the woods. Plenty far
from the sea.

Sunday

Texarkana, 1939
For my Grandmother Coleman

We heard you before we saw you
come pealing across our sky
from the same side as the sunlight
then right over our heads—were you waving
down at us? Who could see you smiling?

A moan above a buzz—
plus me and Sis and the girls
with our fingers cupped over our eyes
chasing after you

damnnear all morning before
you wheeled your way down
to come say hi to us—

least that's half what it sounded like, some tongue
or accent I didn't know. Spanish? All the way from
Spain? No? From where now? Oh—

well you were grand and smiling.
For some reason, less frightening
than other men, I guess. You in your high boots

asking for nothing. Maybe showing off a bit
but hey I'd show off too if I had a flying
machine I could drive across the sky.

Seemed the whole world was asway, swept
in wide gold colors. And that afternoon blue.

The field was your open palm, the day was
my resting hand. For once. And there we were

with you. Got me
caught up in the kind distance of your face, I do
know that language. But mostly I forget the rest—

where were you going? Boy, if I could just take off and go
anywhere—and do it by myself?

I'd be a whole 'nother thang up there in the air, alive
looking down and way out
past Texarkana, past Red Lick, the Depot—Domino!

All this blown land, this blown light—
sure, I'd come back sometime.

Negro Reverend of an All-White Church, Pennsylvania 1941

For my Great Grandfather Ward

Rotten eggs and overripe tomatoes fly
as they turn over in the air, passing
through the broad and open door I built
myself, however many years ago. I watch no longer

immigrant, newly white children dart in and hurl their trash and words
mid-sermon: *spook* and *nigger* and spoiled food tumble in long arcs,
land in the lone aisle of the church I cut, nailed, and raised
with my hard-stretched hands, ever-gentle with the flesh of wood—

Somewhere inside I smile, wildly, remembering
how the Spirit moved their fair-skinned neighbors
to ask *of me* this tabernacle
and I obliged. I have obliged so much so long—I learn

to bid my voice rise just as the foul mess splatters
all over His floor, to cover up the sound, to hold the concentration
of my white faithful looping into new tongues:
this fervor we call grace—*cry holy*—their eyes riding my eyes,
my periphery on their periphery.

                              Lord, help me be what they need
me to be—help me, in my love for You, not to forget
what is eternal of myself. And family. My children of both wives, the Susquehanna
that claimed the burning lungs of my first love. I do not know

what will grow out of us. Of my children and their colors. The end of days
seeps past the doorframe with hate lobbed from small hands, but a flood
of gospel-sweat and prayerful tears forces my eyes up

into the rafters I aligned for You, and them—
There may be no place for me in this river valley,
in this world—I risk belief and call You *home*.

Like wind she passed through the valley

Central Pennsylvania, 1943

A suitcase hidden in the apple trees
at the foot of the orchard hill composed

of one dark blouse, one white; two skirts, one short,
one long; and a shaver's razor blade that belonged

to her father. September disguised. October ignites
sudden color pointing east through leaves. Near sixteen

years she played with sharpness switched open, ran
the old blade along her legs for fun. Mirrors still catch

rough reflections—both sides of the knife. She rushed
away the day of her eighteenth birthday, kept going

past the Susquehanna, past the Capitol. *I decided
on another life*: Philadelphia, the confluence. Light, alone.

Kéloïde

When I stand before thee at the day's end thou shalt see my scars
and know that I had my wounds and also my healing.
~Rabindranath Tagore

Look: anxious badge
bubbling up. Scar

tissue that binds memory to flesh.
See how blood and dirt fused

the bloom. Infection shine
lit the surface

of human water. Birthing
protection. Spalted wood,

splintered home-
grown canoe. Tear

at the scab and
let each tear teach you.

American

After Terrance Hayes

I was afraid of my love for her because of the way she looked into the camera,
like long ago she taught herself to belong there. I want to be more than what you call *rica,*
she says and winks at me. I look off and smile. If you don't know how to be mean
you might be meaner than you think. One night I got near
a borderland called Mania
but Homeland Security crammed the tunnel in my chest with a moon-thick ream
of rain-stained music. Music like a mare
blinking her eyes. My body sung songs that could never be mine. My body ached, tried. I ran
away and stayed 1,000 paces from their guard tower, crouched in the sugar cane
Grandpa swore he'd never touch again, much less harvest. Now I understand: palliative care
is what you give to what you know you love and what you know is dying. Look for your name
in every stare and welcome, in every lost place. Each lie sweet cream
poured fresh from our mouths, dollops left on one another's tongues, ever-melting ice—
lover leaving love, give up. Throw what's left in the skillet, boil the last box of rice,
and teach the little ones how to use the mace
we bought on sale at 7-11 for the medieval struggles around our neighborhood home. America,
I'm not so much afraid to say the words *I love you.* I just don't want to be nice
anymore—I could never trust your aim.

'til I get back

For my Great Grandfather Ford
and for my Dad

George Ford came up $10,000 dollars.

His Great War-veteran, chicken neck-wringing hands
relax, take the shape and weight
of soft black marble, only when he reaches down
to graze the ear of his grandson:
doe-eyed and awestruck. A bud of simple violence.

Young grandpa George finesses a slim roll
of ten crisp $1,000-dollar bills
into that child's wondrous hand—that child will become
my father—and speaks low: *hold this*
'til I get back. Charm. Confidence. The ceremony of the new
grandson and grandfather. Learning the quiet
of one another. Mid-century.

His gait a well-worn labor, turning leaves,
a slick flutter down
the smooth dip in the porch stairs

then road then gone.

I was born in the glint
between them. That wordless ache
that came late, spent, after
life and the money.

My father as a child held impossible green
for him, rolled tight as a sworn secret—
a mute promise built into the blood—
and there was no way for him to know,

the man or the child,
what is born of silence.

Standing Outside a Closed Strip Club

in the Kalamazoo woods
at 5am two
strippers (who)
just (got) off
work save my life

and give me a ride downtown and
smoke me down (out)
in 8 hours I will bless
the food at my childhood
friend's wedding

"IR cuck"

So this sensation
of watching
your booty being
watched by a white
man, mid-sexing
his wife, his girlfriend,

his love?—She asks you
to have her—for him?
His quietness
as he looks all over you   -
feels nothing like
an American

accident, feels like
more than
any internet media
player—just about
damn near the same
as I feel any other day.

Draft Night: Nautical Brothas Association

For Zion, Ja, RJ, Matisse, and the rest of us

I see the tall, young black men crying on national tv,
bowing their heads weeping, even sobbing.
Their voices gasp and spill, stutter and fly
as they reach for the crutch of word and steady sound.

Broad shoulders jitter and sputter as their muscles
make movements I have never seen before
and only felt happening inside myself
while weeping wildly in a car on the side of the road
with someone I love. Or alone. In a dark, wet field, tired,
surrounded by the company of night.
(In an empty gym once, too, and in a foreign quiet
living room . . . but where am I now?—I distract myself.) Here,

buoyed by the night, bathed blue and American in soft electric light:
I watch these men on live tv with wonder.
What blackness is becoming is releasing

some stitch of pain, some wall of fear
to find our way to unknown pains and fears, yes, but
I saw so many young giants in the culture crying, letting go
of tears of joy and something else
floating away, out in the open, in front of teenaged strangers
donning jerseys stitched with their new cities and names,
in front of black and white women, young and old,
in front of uneasy white men in suits and money, in front
of bright screens, microphones, and the silent eyes of cameras.
I always knew there was something blue inside of freedom.

My guess is we won't sink, even though there's no rest as we
crest with the water. There's a river flooding the city inside us,
there's a surge bloody as history, silty as time, leaking past
the sandbags, crossing the makeshift shores that keep the kin

I love. I watch and feel this American spectacle the way I imagine
a cruise ship custodian watches and feels the ocean at night
as he mops and shines the deck, biding his time.

Glitch Miracles Here

After Casey Gerald

Lonely, but more
importantly, dangerous. The process a path
                    of going, of being
                    a symbol. You
                    take—you,
a kid, a kid like me:
from Forgotten,
                 and send, put, cover
                 him on a cliff
and on and on
                 this stage—it allows
          us to imagine this country, to
          pretend—most people are

          a belt conveyed from Nothing
          to Nowhere. No—
                 Quiet Thing, you see—

you see: *I'm a Glitch*
in the American Machine, which
         works off this Fantasy
called the American Dream.

        As long as,
        as long as

I don't confess
the world keeps
ticking. How little, how much
sense
this illusion:
                But I become—
                Liar.
                        But I become—

The Broken Man's Permission

A crocodile slips its earth-toned body
back into the river, in silence, violence down
and in this nightness

I cannot see the water. With fear
I am alone. Slick rocks smile thin anonymous light, they lie

about what I am. I see and try to hold
my body in my body, trace a vein
from the base of my palm through

the crook of my elbow, armpit, home—home
makes no sense. I've given up on what I know.

This blindness is a mirror dissolving
back to sand worn hollow, where
every sound is amplified. I want to be the crocodile's

stomach that is my father, teeth
that are my mother, vertebrae

that aggregate the spine that are loves, knuckled
angles casing nerves. It's me wading around
inside, mouth open. A humid numbness, dense

beneath the undertow: hands that coax and claim
my scaled neck, soothe and pull

each knotted shoulder. I give in to a third of moon caught
in cloud, its orange-grey halo drawn away
from everything I've ever known. A curse and prayer

to go unchanged within this water, my movement
foreign, a rootless gurgle, flit of river vines

caging the dwindling
river's brutal bed, the gorge, flushed
with new food: the blue heron's bone-flight collapsed,

tangled feathers along the mudglut bank's
saliva, lifting like shame in the open.

We Placed Our Fear in a Wicker Basket

2011 drunk, walking around
shook down   gravity. Right hand aimless
as city noise, as night, left   hand on wet brick, trying
to braid these fingers   into graffiti, falling in
love with it. One more minute of eye   contact away
from unbuckling our pants together

right here, on a 3am riproaring street   but far away
enough, really   just a few blocks   south, between
a metal doorway and black, leaning trees. I slip

inside you, push almost patiently
and listen to   the sounds you make,
your hands that reach   back for my ass, pull me

in. I'm kissing your hair   your neck, holding you up
against the rusted metal door. Neither of us
on the lookout, alert for trouble.   What do we care

about? What do we know   about each
other? I knew I walked by   the same
site—the shrill monument masked by time
and emptiness—three years later   in broad daylight,
palm to palm   with another woman, one I love,
your face   almost blurring me.

Stained Glass Speaks

For/After Robert Hayden

[BREED]

Deliver me and my mouth—
deliver
me and my shadow's poise

my fearful quiet
yawning holy structure—failure

dismember
me and my commodity-identity-history:
another busted hull tilted toward the sky—

flotsam of belonging scudding
this way and that in the warm tide

this tethered riot this
anthem this hazardous
life full of whys in its waves

so that the brittle and backlit curse
lifted up [is that what we be?] might be

shattered into tongues
might crick collision unmeasured
in shards that teem

like water—so bright that broken glass
in me falling might be the chorus finding

its scarlet rhythm—the confluence
of each voiced lie and love [ain't we
always in between?] as they gush

then mist into the air, misremembered—over
the edge of how, the throat of no

[HARD TEAR]

Tremor in the diamond memory
a needle dipped in music

more than muscle more than blood:
helpless, contagious. Sing:
sink where we believe.

Each mind inside mine a wide-eyed scale
on the sleek dark flank of history:

the exotic beast turns, rises
on its haunches, bleets, spews
ecstasy and anxiety in order

to drown the empires in their continents
as they thrash and spread—who's

surprised by the sharpness of mouths
how they cut through
belief?

[TAR]

What can I do but enter
naked now and lie down
in this raw lair
of nectar and threat,
sicksweet amalgam
of shifting
heaving

borders, once again my   black-
patterned 200 plus pounds 6-foot self   conjuring
swollen roots that roam forever
beneath us beneath sky
cored through
the deep work of what I am—

what you are—in spite of
ourselves
we swallow something
other than air—
[don't forget
to breathe]
whose harsh blued angle
of each america in us

[TORN CORE]

Naked we stood and watched
The honeybee

Fling itself against the dirty glass
Window in the shower

For what felt like hours, but it had to
Be less than even one

Before it drowned in the steam
Or just got tired, spilling

Down, swiped tiny paws not paws,
Soft, in our eyes, and slippery

Against the chipped wooden border. Our
Sex at rest a different kind

Of body open. You tried, I tried,
To gently touch and bend

Our body over, to keep going but I
Kept listening for its buzzing

Until one of us got out. Then both.

[TREACHERY]

There is
a[n open] door.

[DARE]

Awake and made   in air, I leave

the branches, the seashore,   the other spirits   living

silent and long. A reflection   blinded,

set boldly, a bower   jewel and drum   and home. I am

my country, a wind stumbling   above Columbus, a palm

beyond ashes anchors   my return. I chose this

night boat adrift on yesterday,   decay, and memory.   Forgot I had

gathered pilgrimed sand   in my dark hands   from men whose May

may shatter me. Still. Hallelujah   fluttering from the crimson

fringes of my earth,   weary,   singing sleet.

[SEED]

skin the wet color
of ghost-ripped trees

their fog
their lilt
[bet]ween me.

[REACH]

Would you believe me if I warned you
I'm dangerous? Do you think you would agree
when I say I'm never certain, always plural, and
no longer care to know? I spend my lives looking

at you, aiming to believe. You comment on my eyes,
the shape of them, and I wonder where
I learned to hide. Or is it instinct? The unlearned
unleashed. The pull pushed back. Faith spun

the roots that keep the leaves. Gaunt flags of seaweed
in the hoary Atlantic sing our [nightgreen] song
of to and fro. Painting wave after wave, steadily
down. Here. Where all roots look alien to me.

There's foreign and then there's unknown—
There's fear and then there's the dark.

Stronghold

Hollow home swaddled in smoke—war-
readied, mortared dense and rogue
against whose ancient cavernous
scars and holes. Cement body barren
except vigilant fluorescence, ghosts of soldiers

blink and yawn in silver light. My mind of midnight
fog swallows up its base and height. Collision
becomes construction. Collapse becomes
mass production. Notice: the kingdom has its own
body born from fear, still slippery. Witness its absence,

its silence: a new wall thick with closed eyes
clenched as lungs clench breath—the last
General rushes to hoist a cracked bell
and the sound of death floods
the wrist of land he cannot own.

Life and Death Grow Round

After Ross Gay, Patrick Rosal, and Gerard Manley Hopkins

Melting ice falls on the tin like
A drummer boy falls on his drum:
Rhythm—staccato, palpitation, thump,—

Thump-thump:—I am
Grieving the living song
And so extending it, us, you

    *

Don't believe me? Trust *grief*
Is the altar for listening

To the beginning of the world.
Tectonic in the grief: love, gratitude

Forgotten thank yous shook hands *shook foil*
All the while the drop the water embraces—is—us.

"Do you accept Negroes?"

Variations on a Letter to a White/Church outside Detroit (ca. 1967)

Do you accept these ghosts?
Do you accept need grows?
Do you accept seeds groan?
Do you accept grief flows?

Do you accept pleas, honed?
Do you accept screams slowed?
Do you accept teeth sold?
Do you accept, mouth closed?

Do you accept thieved bones?
Do you accept seized gold?
Do you accept leased coast?
Do you accept trees moan?

Do you accept these holes?
Do you accept we know?

"It appears the gift could not be refused."

Trapped in the speed of the highway
the white seabird flew too low

against the sky. The shrill wing clipped
and spiraled out of life like

a sudden broken spell. Mute precision: god
in the oncoming headlight behind me

solemn. At roughly 80 miles
an hour, the hollow-boned body

spit into the air before careening
toward the roaring ground. All of this

quick and lonely as I watch
new death in the burnished frame

of my rearview mirror. I keep going.
Watch a man decide to live inside the blade

of prayer that is his body. The country
became what countries become and I was

one black man forced to drive
inside it. When I look back

through my mind, the white seabird still
whirls, raw and at an angle

fitted by the blunt machine of grief.
Its death was a gift in its precision—

chance gorges on another life
and our new wound blooms.

Wilma Rudolph Contemplates Her Stride

My legs, my legs—
my bones remember when they could not walk.
Once I was a child, bedridden in a simple room. But
when the Savior say, "Rise."
you rise.

And then I taught myself to run—
tore the muscle fiber of my thighs a thousand times
on a thousand stairs. All those stone-stepped stadiums,
how they sag and lean in the bruised light
before morning,
the pale-blue chill of it. The field below
just at the end of darkness, a hushed, wet green
where old and new sweat mix in with the dew.

My bones remember nights
filled with more and more thousands:
endless practices and track meets, the painful seconds
that form and fill 100, 200, 400
meters, and every word from Coach Temple.

But I remember most the stairs:
empty—then brimming with people.
So many idolizing eyes
covet the strength I built into my body.
Tearing down a white-lined lane
in front of crowds shouting languages I'll never know . . .
yes, I do remember Rome. Summer 1960. I do.
Three gold, world records.
                              No, I am not your "black gazelle."
I am Woman. Mother. Southerner. Teacher.
Hometown Activist. Changemaker. *What else? Who*

keeps chasing me? What am I running from—to?
But I know how to still my mind. I trust
the rage in my training—
I know what made my legs
and I still climb my stairs.

Regeneration

Changeful ancient blood—

                Again and again in the arc

        Of my body, fought with it to get

                Through water: past it—me. We

Gone breathe our way home.

Meditation

inhale, hold, exhale

Memory is my wristwatch
The sun is the top button of my shirt
Today I sacrifice myself to brightness

Today I am morning made
Only, already, always, anyway
Another interval before and after night

Copper and clear blue, a blot rising
In the face of all of this
I hereby swear by the mundane beautiful—

Night is my wristwatch
The sun is the top button of my memory
I sacrifice my morning to brightness

Today I am hereby today
Anyway, always, already, only
Another blue interval, clear before and after

All this blot the shirt of myself made
I swear the mundane beautiful is
Rising in the copper of my face—

3

*Three levels underground I pushed upon a heavy metal door
marked "Danger" and descended into a noisy, dimly lit room.
There was something familiar about the fumes that filled the air
and I had just thought pine, when a high-pitched Negro voice rang out
above the machine sounds.*
RALPH ELLISON'S INVISIBLE MAN

Who hears another side of home?

Streets speak if we listen to
those of us who river through
but, listen: liquid language leaves
waterways and bells, bridges
ambassadors and isles, miles and salt
mines and sky lines, lodges corridors,
heartsick bronze fists and plazas
cast and wild-wooded, grand boulevards
full of static verticality. Were you
woodward there with me when we
watched love change—I watched love
change me. Generations from the late
night rust-red River Rouge foundry
to the early morning loading docks
of Eastern Market, broad black hands
loved and cursed and prayed, made
a living that made years that long
after made me long after they
left and didn't leave. Hands unpacked
three Souths, unpacked Back East, right
here: let kin roam in notes in lost letters
cursive in tabernacle pews and juke
joints and valleys of paradise
obliterated by postwar concrete. Migration
buries seeds. Believe the domain beneath
interstate highway cloverleaf
butterfly ramps still speaks
imminently through me. What we
can't say, what we can't see. Where
faith and survival branch and break
out of plots on former family
streets: Seyburn. Van Dyke. Mack.

Greenlawn. Burlingame. Outer
Drive. Ditmar. Ditmar. Ditmar.
South Boulevard. Telegraph.
Oneida. Adams. Somehow
Savoie. Off of Evergreen. How
many miles—Home and
never home. What we
can't say, what we can't be.

iv. Return to Sunset Point (Belle Isle, Detroit)

The Mapmaker Scouts a Border

I dream a dream that dreams back at me.
~ Toni Morrison

The gateway is the drug. Each edge I see
in me's a living thing, a yes

that rustles the throat to
find the mouth.

No burns up tomorrow,
lights gasoline's song

falling on highway wildflowers—pressed
for morning rain. Swing wide,

swing low—chariot or scythe—I
promise you

I'm only half-ghost. I've felt them
in my face, I've heard them

in my voice blurring into yours—there's
a flag of wild emptiness

patterned on my skin. Now evening
storm spills itself and fills me

up as night consumes the order. Hijacked horses
hide inside the way they run

away. So always
I'll come back

to see if you are safe, to see
what waves of us were left and what was made. I

watch for movement
in the soft-lit rooms behind your face.

Driving I-80 East as My Grandfather Did, Half a Century Before

I've come back, left hand at twelve
on the steering wheel the same way
my Grandfather came back. Chromed out
Detroit muscle, four-door Cutlass Supreme
handwashed, set to shine on

arrival after the Turnpike, no radio reception then or now when
my Mother, his daughter, my Uncle, his son,
my love he heard of
but never met, ride at rest around me. I drive us the way
he taught my Uncle to go, map

unfolding in his head and in his voice—
he passed away before he had a chance to meet my love, years
warring with pancreatic cancer until
October, late evening, gone.
I was South, far away. On my phone in a hallway

I said a prayer, spoke with family voices, remembered
how near the end he told me, *You need your own*
personal relation with God. I had one then. And I do now, driving us
up the old paved spine to his hometown, up river in the Susquehanna
Valley, engine punching through downpour before

brightness. This summer together, everyone still
asleep except me as the radio crackles back to life—
Motown static creviced in these Pennsylvania
hills. Family Back East, we're coming
to see you again.

Late in the feature film

When I turn the movie on, the young American hero's
finally beginning to recognize himself, finally
accepting that mystic cosmic ritual of post-almost defeat

coronation with luscious synchronous sound
roaring in the background. The music, more than
the scene, is a coming

coal blue-green and muddy brown
waterfall out of sight up ahead. We (the plural anonymous) are
already in it, the pull

already lifting the weight we felt. His smooth
touch made just rough enough by the tear of narrative.
The gravel in his voice is sex.

I'm just a gendered being sitting on the couch enthralled
and shook by my easy thrall in all of it. Watching
him with women, how expressions skim across

bodies—now the rush picks up and I'm stuck
in the final thirty minutes of
this feature, caught in my personal darkness, soaked

in my byzantine clutter of personal effects, their faint scent
of a life before this one. Other times, people. All of it
reminding me that I have come

here along some far way through
relations and places, jobs and languages, scuttled blueprints
of belief, paper-mâchéd to make memory—identity. The swelling

hero on screen wants blood—but first: he must sit
in a midday highway diner booth, must listen
across from an oracular child

who dips a finger into a loopy maze,
babbles and traces a path on a kids-eat-free placemat map
colored in busted crayon. Red. Yellow. Blue. Destiny

for the hero and child as characters, as actors, the crew workers,
producers, parents, handlers, agents, and pages, etc. and me, plus
whoever else watches, whoever else leans

and loafs in their personal darkness, given over
to the nighttime tick of anonymous revelry—all of us must wonder:
How did I get here? Did I choose this for me?

The answer matters less than the wonder,
collectively. I feel it. Here we are
in some crescendo, swept up in the signature music,

fantastical,
possibly
deadly.

Twitter Poem: In the Year of Our Lord

Where were you when his body became
birdsong? A blue-bright unseen
fragment in the sky? Did you come
running? Did you hide?

#NPRpoetry #nationalpoetrymonth #myfirstTweet

Life Inside the Clock

The kettle tilts like a broken Earth,
axis leaning over the oven's gas
flame. Amber residue slips
the flavor of animal fat into water
but does not make it soup.
(We know what is and is not food.)
Watch the ancestor watch
the kettle the way a child
watches a mother's sleep
consume the room—the dream
seen from outside of it. There
is a zeroed spirit wheeling in the air
like liquid glass thickening
between her gaze and where
I want her slow work to lead
you. To lead me. The eternal curve
in her back is the dark muscle
in mine. Her hands died
and became my hands. Her song
seethes and lights the burnished bones
that cage my mouth. I learned I had
her brother's laugh—still
have. Distilled, always watching. Above
the sky blue lilt of gas fire. Before
I can hear that simple whistling—
and while I know I cannot
see inside the kettle: I make myself
believe a single shrill pocket of air
tighter than my father's fist
is crawling now, escaping up
the black insides
of its small and temporary room.

Catarata que no cae

Uno tiene que tener paciencia;
eso quizás entiendo ahora—

lo veo más claro con cada gota de mi vida:
que la cascada no caiga

ni que la garganta caiga
ni que caiga la boca del río

si me muevo solo dentro del momento—
Acá me presento.

A Fire She Loved

For Pontiac, For Detroit, (1997, and always)

The whiskey slipped into the cut
between her first finger and thumb
as she raised the lowball glass. She
didn't stop to rinse it, didn't wince until
her long pull was already midway down
her throat. A fire she loved. Heavier, warmer
than the feel on her face of the oven
as she worked through the night
into early morning, halfway-drunk
in that ancient basement kitchen,
her former high school's lunchroom.
An industrial oven. Wide enough for five pies,
dark tins as broad as her father's open hands.

Meat pies or fruit pies, but most often her famous
sweet potato. The smell of such sweetness
as she lifted and leaned mixed with her body's sweat
and was at first sacred, then nauseating, then nothing at all
once it became the habit of her life. Everyday, unrelenting
reality. She would sing
under her breath spirituals
that surprised her about herself. She was long grown
beyond the church, but she remembered. This before-morning:

> *No weapon, formed against me, shall prosper . . .*
> *It won't work, no weapon—*

Almost absurd, but not, as she slides
the cutting board and trusted knife away, into
the potato skin tatters, and takes a bigger caramel swig,
considering the smoke of it, smiling to herself, lately. She wonders
not how she got down there, but why she stayed
down there. And did the work
she did, feeding so many, on her own.

He Won't Give Up, I Won't Give Up

(2008)

A woman's hand balances my own, guides me as I
        stumble like a lost child

in a hurt state. I drink and drown in what
                so much of me won't stop wanting. Looking
around a loud dark

room alive with eyes, eyes alive with room for my same kind
                      of loss, of want. Our loss:
a bucket of hunted fish left out in rain

        *

        accidentally, us, swallowed in sound—
Earth's wet falling

back to Earth again. I spill
        as pain spills into life. As change grows

heavier, harder
        to hold and more
impatient. I worry

I've already ruined me. If I lie to myself, to whom else
am I lying? Soft with time, I know
                  more than remember

        *

the way one old man falls
          asleep, drunk at our kitchen table,
his head somehow finds relief

          in the same crooked angle
as the parking lot basketball hoop I loved,
          that I actually loved, even more after

someone had thrown something too hard
          through it—I still see
a chunk of concrete—

its plexiglass had a jagged hole
          I shot a ball in silence through

once more
          then put it all
down. So late now. Sighing. I'll always hold

                    *

                    that old man's slumped
          head lolling behind my eyes, keep feeling
pitiful for both of us, our silences: my lateness

          not in seeing but in telling.
I can't forget how I wanted to love

my fists as a kid, small brown eggs
beginning to tremble in a pot
          of shallow water.

My Big Brother, Oblivion

(2016)

In paradise I poised my foot above the boat and said:
Who prayed for me?
~ James Wright

The gloss-red circle that is the bottom

      of the beat-up Solo cup begins to tilt

back down toward the ground

      and his nose then his mouth

            come back

into view—the pupils of his syrupy eyes never leave

      the question of my face. I can't quite tell

how old he is, how young he is—

            he pulls

      a long thick puff then a quick sharp one

at the end, before a rush of white smoke

      spills up to heaven from his dark lips, before

he says, *You betta hold on tight to life, brotha.*

Tread—Gambol

To live in my infinitive
Skeletal echo's resound

Through the thick blood roaring
Through mine small reckless being

In its furtive no and obsessive yes
In its thud and stomp and gone dance

***

But who sees those who go
unseen? Pushed forward

by death until we are
planted with those who cede

sun in some souls' triangulation, some
heart-claimed delta. Change escapes

from pockets, slick river silt that carries
us with no need to say I am.

"South of the North, yet north of the South, lies the City of a Hundred Hills"

~W.E.B. Du Bois

Peering past the promise I
          half-roused the soil—
    the tinkle rattle
          of life swelled

               until Atlanta and the Alleghenies
          awakened, aroused and listening
             to sea, city, weeds and bread,
      bitterness, sweat. Live

haunted, see vision, feel conquered
          yet, Black—Dared. Us
People of the Turned Future,
          of Purple Kingdom, of Gateway, of Web

          so crowned with cunning, and stretched, and
      striving—Perhaps
          christened Wild, startled
again. Named not Temple, but Gospel.

Fear one-half question racing America, dire
          land, gold whim, stooping fault,
     find. I was no idle wilderness—
          after the re-birth and between heavy

          wings all red
             tempted,
    half-forgotten, under
             kindliness, carelessness, lead.

Verdant, Overlush

A density of thieves rocked into his breathing
so he is powder now. Slowly
his native city's tech-sick geometry
unlit, powered down. Asphalt
melting its forgiveness, *You know me*

        whispers wilderness. And who
        we are, and what we do, each way we
        want begins to bleed over
        an acre of need. Flooding. *Hold on*
        goes the night I am here forever holding

The Flag Eater

I woke up believing
I had swallowed a flag whole,

discolored and withered
the bright shapes of its symbols, only
half-digesting it

so that a dark chord was being
pushed and pulled through my intestines'

rootlike strength. I could feel
its strange length thin and twisted
within me. I felt ancient and alarmed as I sat down

on the toilet in my quiet bathroom
and shat and coughed and exhaled in peace. Released

myself with all abandon
until I stood up and looked down
to see the flag turned human colors,

delicate and veined as vegetable leaves.
My eyes felt clearer. My body balanced as I blinked

at the diaphanous flag on the other side
of its invention. Wondering
what nutrients from it were left in me, how

it had survived, transformed
deep brown and soft gold cast

through the warm darkness of my carnal being.
There was a pleasure
as I flushed my secret.

I took what was not food
and made it feed me. I did not choke.

The animal of me was in control.
I thought I'd never need to eat another flag
and slowly washed my hands, considering my surface

in the mirror. I closed my eyes
a moment, then went about my day.

Cough

(2020)

　　　　　This broken glass so bright in me
　　　　　I wheeze, I breathe, I bleed, look
　　　　　down at the sink colors and gleam

in the drain. Life together with death
gifts us miracles. Somehow, still
here. The apartment at night shook

　　　　　until we found one morning, still until
　　　　　I teetered with support beams, wood
　　　　　in sounds around us creaks gravity—

pressure clutters my skull, but
what hangs, what balances
sharp from the end of the plumb

　　　　　line held vertical and air enough
　　　　　in me, these feather lungs, this life, to
　　　　　make blood new, keep going.

When I hear my mama sing

an altar pulses open: some ancient bloodlove unfurls
what breath remembers: my body of her body and all
we come from and come from and come from, how
each of us curves with the world, blown like a leaf

swells from its tree: green urge, earthdark, branching
seconds bend, browning. The flesh of wood forever fills
me with her sound of abundant rain: how the world she
rounds reminds me what I would be if yes, if

yes: I trust the feeling pouring through the sound,
pouring through as many openings in me as holes
in our steel blue strainer: the family tool holds time
again and again in hands beneath our kitchen sink, ready

to caress the mesh: hold and let fall water. If I
listen for my body living I hear who I am.

The idea of water

For A. B.

waves filled her first thought

the wildness of falling

down and through

on her way as she felled

his every burning tree

until his very stillness

stopped into bloom

after bloom of rain

on skin on night

on wind poured quick

into smoke and nearby light

until the looking

that was the working

grew sentenceless

each phrase and fragment

a fragrance escaping, no—

a human scent, its

laws of sweat and love

and fear whispering the air

careening into

heavy droplets

flooded open

then leaving

a *cavern kindness*

suddenly our own

grown crimson with

evening then

oceanic after blue

"Before I Let Go"

When something inside the ear opens in
                                        welcome, the body moves out into a mood
                with gumption and delight

                toward a clearing in the bar called a dance
floor: a narrow alley of glass walls glowing
                with key lime-colored light. We do this

                                        fast or slow. Maze somewhere smiling,
                                                as new friends glide together
                in the waterfall of the Hustle. So many of us

                went head and got down. I was just one
more of the black beautiful sauntering and smiling
                over a shoulder, fingertips reaching down

        to touch the floor, to flick a nickel up
                                        from the ground, shoulder blades loose, lifting
        a knee like the moon's rise, for the first time

                after how many years of pandemic—I was suddenly grateful
                                        to know my body remembered
                how to gently move

        into the rhythm of a human space, how
to float on waves. Sometimes I was in front, sometimes
                                        I was behind. I learned again to pour

myself into water. Of many ages we were also wind

      lifting white curtains from a nighttime open

            window, exiting the room. I was not as disillusioned

     as I thought I was. As the synced sound of the song

            faded we laughed in dim light

    flooded with one another. Then we went where we needed to flow.

Two Links in a June Chain

For my Dad

You weave in me my many names:
Chaser, Leaning Ace of Spades, Decadent
Sling of Inertia, Strange Hope, Slang, Wave,

     River Between Two Countries, Shoulder,
     Young Croon, Boat, Aging Smile, Throat
     Clearer Extraordinaire,

Heavy Hand, Forgotten
Prince of Silence, Grown
Son and Careful Child,
Abstract Future Father—

     You believed me into being. We
     breathe to be equinox. You and what you have
     but did not choose, you and what you chose, and
     what you gave of your body, but could not save. Still

your eyes are more than names for me,
two slow blooms of long-drawn smoke.

     I imagine a continent, and then a cliff
     cut down into the earth. I am the black echo

of all our shared silences. (I know
now: I can thank you) I trust you
to be you and nothing else. I feel

your blood rising in my body
alongside something that needs
no name, no word or look or walk, just
a truth worn smooth. And

what is true but nameless
knows no beginning or end

NOTES

"*i. Figures One Through Two*" This erasured handmade map was crafted through and over Samuel Penniman Bates's chapter on the 25th United States Colored Regiment in his *History of Pennsylvania volunteers, 1861-5* (first published in 1869). My great, great, great grandfather served in the 25th U.S. Colored Regiment in the United States Civil War.

"Time and place have had their say," The epigraph of section one is borrowed from Zora Neale Hurston's autobiography *Dust Tracks on a Road.*

"I could always just hear somebody running" This poem learned its title from Fred Moten, who spoke this sentence while in conversation with Saidiya Hartman at Duke University in 2016 for their series, *The Black Outdoors: Humanities Futures after Property and Possession.*

"I Know It Was the Blood" This poem borrows its title from the Black gospel hymn of the same name. See Mahalia Jackson's performances of the hymn for further reference. The poem's epigraph quotes Etheridge Knight's poem, "The Idea of Ancestry."

"ii. Battle Flag: 'Strike for God and [. . .] 25th United States Colored Troops (1863-1865)'" image information: On verso: Photographed by B.F. Reimer, No. 624 Arch Street, Philada. In album: [U.S. army officers and other persons of the Civil War period / John White Geary, comp. 1861-1865], no. 135, surrogate p. 34 (lower left).

"iii. In front of Philadelphia City Hall . . ." photograph by Aaron Coleman.

". . . lit with red life, / the holler of survivor's blood . . ." quotes Aracelis Girmay's poem "After" in *The Black Maria.*

"Kéloïde" According to the Online Etymology Dictionary, the word keloid in English is "also *cheloid*, 1854, from French *kéloïde*, from Greek *khēlē* 'crab claw, talon, cloven hoof' + -*oidēs*." See also "-oid: word-forming element meaning 'like, like that of, thing like a _____,' from Latinized form of Greek -*oeidēs* (three syllables), from *eidos* 'form,' related to *idein* 'to see,' *eidenai* 'to know;' . . . Often implying an incomplete or imperfect resemblance to the thing indicated."

The epigraph of "Kéloïde," "When I stand before thee at the day's end, thou shalt see my scars and know that I had my wounds and also my healing" is borrowed from Rabindranath Tagore's "Stray Birds" (1916) self-translated by Tagore.

"A m e r i c a n" This poem owes a debt to Terrance Hayes's anagram-like form in *Hip Logic* in the section "A Gram of &s."

"Draft Night: Nautical Brothas Association" Its epigraph, which begins *For Zion, Ja, RJ, Matisse . . .* , includes the names of several Black players from Australia, Canada, and the United States selected in the first round of the 2019 National Basketball Association Draft.

"Glitch Miracles Here" This poem reworks language from a Casey Gerald interview regarding his memoir *There Will Be No Miracles Here* on NPR's *Weekend Edition* (Sept. 30th, 2018):

> "It's a very lonely path. But more importantly, it's a very dangerous path. I write in the book about the process of going from a kid to being a symbol. You know, you take a kid like me from a forgotten world like Oak Cliff, and you send him off to Yale and Harvard Business School, and you put him on the cover of magazines, and you put him on the stage at TED. And it allows us to imagine or to pretend that there is not a conveyor belt leading most people in this country from nothing to nowhere.
>
> You see, I'm a glitch in the American machine, which works off this fantasy called the American dream. But as long as I'm quiet about that, as long as I don't confess how little sense this journey makes, then the world can keep on ticking. But I become a liar. I become an illusion."

"Stained Glass Speaks" draws "nightgreen" from Robert Hayden's poem, "The Diver" where Hayden writes ". . . Swiftly descended / into canyon of cold/night-green emptiness./ Freefalling, weightless/as in dreams of / wingless flight . . .'"

"It appears the gift could not be refused" borrows its title from Jack Gilbert's poem, "In Dispraise of Poetry," the first poem in his first book, *Views of Jeopardy*.

"Three levels underground I pushed upon a heavy metal door marked 'Danger' and descended into a noisy, dimly lit room. There was something familiar about the fumes that filled the air and I had just thought pine, when a high-pitched Negro voice rang out above the machine sounds," the epigraph to section three, is borrowed from Ralph Ellison's *Invisible Man*.

"iv. Return to Sunset Point (Belle Isle, Detroit)" photograph by Aaron Coleman.

"The Map Mapmaker Scouts a Border" The poem's epigraph, "I dream a dream that dreams back at me" quotes Florens in Toni Morrison's novel, *A Mercy*.

"Twitter Poem: In the Year of Our Lord" was my first tweet on April 15th, 2018.

"My Big Brother, Oblivion" The poem's epigraph, "In paradise I poised my foot above the boat and said: Who prayed for me?" quotes James Wright's poem, "Father."

"Life and Death Grow Round" With thanks to Ross Gay's meditation on grief in his essay "Grief Suite (Falling Apart: The Thirteenth Incitement)" in *Inciting Joy* that led me to Patrick Rosal's *Atang: an altar for listening to the beginning of the world*. With love to Gerard Manley Hopkins's "God's Grandeur." Shook foil!

"Catarata que no cae" I might translate this title in English as "Unfalling waterfall" or "Waterfall that does not fall." I did not feel compelled to translate myself back into English in this poem.

"A Fire She Loved" This poem is dedicated to all the Black matriarchs I've been blessed to know and love.

"South of the North, yet north of the South, lies the City of a Hundred Hills" draws its title from the first sentence of W.E.B. Du Bois's essay, "Of the Wings of Atalanta" in *The Souls of Black Folk*. The poem is an erasure of Du Bois's essay.

"The idea of water" The italicized phrase, "cavern kindness," is borrowed from Gwendolyn Brooks's poem "A Lovely Love."

"Before I Let Go" shouts out the title of the Maze song (and Beyoncé remix!) of the same name, which first appeared on their 1981 album *Live from New Orleans*.

ACKNOWLEDGMENTS

This manuscript was developed with the support of a National Endowment for the Arts Creative Writing Fellowship.

I want to extend my deep gratitude and appreciation to the following publications for publishing poems that appear in this collection (or previous versions of them):

Academy of American Poets *Poem-a-Day* series, *Boston Review*, *Callaloo: A Journal of African Diaspora Arts & Letters*, *Chicago Review*, *Chicago Quarterly Review*, *Columbia Journal* [Columbia University, NY], *Columbia Poetry Review* [Columbia College Chicago], *ERGON: Greek/American and Diaspora Arts & Letters*, *Four Way Review*, *Guesthouse*, *Jet Fuel Review*, *The Massachusetts Review*, *The Missouri Review*, *On the Seawall*, *Plume*, Pulitzer Arts Foundation *Together/Apart 100 Boots Poetry* Series, *Raleigh Review*, *The Rumpus*, *The Slowdown* podcast, *Spoon River Poetry Review*, *Under a Warm Green Linden*, *Vinyl*, *What Rough Beast*, and *wildness*.

The final years of writing this book were a time of both profound grief and profound gratitude in my life. I moved back to my home state of Michigan to join the faculty at the University of Michigan, a short drive away from most of my family in Metro-Detroit. And at the same time, many of my family members and friends transitioned to be with our ancestors these past few years. Losing so many loved ones has changed me and taken a toll on my health as we've tried to honor them, carry on, and care for those of us still living on this side. It's changed my relationship to life, death, and the systemic violences that threaten our lives. I'm grateful to Four Way Books for their compassion and flexibility during some very difficult years.

About half of the poems in *Red Wilderness* engage family histories and tales of my ancestors (what I've come to call "ancestral poems") so this work evolved new dimensions of grief and praise as it neared completion. I hope this creative effort honors all those who have joined our ancestors with love, respect, and gratitude for my life and our future generations of kin (both blood and chosen). Blessings to Thelma Ward, Richard M. Ward, Michael Bolivar, Tai Mitchell, Hank Mitchell, Cousin Chuck, Uncle Dewey, Richard Anderson, Dwayne Rayford, and all our loved ones beyond this life.

Thank you to the National Endowment for the Arts for the financial support that helped keep me and this project afloat during the first years of the pandemic. I also want to thank Cave Canem for sacred community and the creative fuel to keep going, wherever we find ourselves. Thank you to the Comparative Literature departments, MFA programs, English departments, African American Studies departments, and library communities at the University of Michigan and Washington University in St. Louis for communal support and our many generative conversations.

There are so many brilliant people I want to thank for the impact they've had on me and these poems in one kind way or creative way or another. Heartfelt thanks to Hanif Abdurraqib, Eric Aiken, Lauren K. Alleyne, Baba Badji, Victoria Bamn, Mary Jo Bang, Espelencia Baptiste, Lyndon Barrois Jr., Layla Benitez-James, VersAnnette Blackman-Bosia, Tommye Blount, Bénédicte Boisseron, Daniel Borzutzky, Catherine Brown, Jericho Brown, rebecca brown, Dominic Chambers, Andy Chen, Jon Cho-Polizzi, Cassandra Cleghorn, Doris L. Coleman, Shonnese C.L. Coleman, Kristiana Rae Colón, Nandi Comer, Kwame Dawes, Tyree Daye, Patrick Donnelly, Timothy Donnelly, Carlina Duan, Addoley Dzegede, Frieda Ekotto, Jen Everett, Ross Gay, Jacqui Germain, Shine Goodie, Linda Gregerson, Rav Grewal-Kok, Marwa Helal, Rage Hezekiah, Kelly Hoffer, Jerrod Howlett, Ignacio Infante, Kahlil Robert Irving, Tyehimba Jess, A. Van Jordan, Douglas Kearney, Lydia Kelow-Bennett, Edgar Kunz, Cortney Lamar Charleston, Dana Levin, Jane Huffman, Aida Levy-Hussen, Delsa Lopez, Liz London, Tariq Luthun, Hannah Matheson, Khaled Mattawa, Philip Matthews, Aurielle Marie, Félipe Martínez, William J. Maxwell, Nathan McClain, Charleen McClure, Peggy McCracken, Dante Micheaux, Jonah Mixon-Webster, Faisal Mohyuddin, Cheswayo Mphanza, Ryan Murphy, Umniya Najaer, Yvonne Osei, Sope Oyelaran, Benjamin Paloff, Mithil Pandhi, Patrick Patillo, Maura Pellettieri, Carl Phillips, Todd Portnowitz, Yopie Prins, David Pryor, Erin Quick, Renée Ragin Randall, Justin Phillip Reed, L. Renée, Katherine Simóne Reynolds, Aaron Robertson, Joy Priest, Roger Reeves, Martha Rhodes, Dalychia Saah, Niloofar Sarlati, Diane Seuss, Brenda Shaughnessy, Evie Shockley, Aisha Sabatini Sloan, Jennifer Sperry Steinorth, William Stroebel, SaraEllen Strongman, Chandler Tann, Sarah Tisdale, Maurice Tracy, Antoine Traisnel, Paul Tran, Jess Walker,

Silke-Maria Weineck, Phillip B. Williams, El Williams III, Josh Wilson, Eileen Wilson-Oyelaran, Colin Witherspoon, Amy Wright, and Rafia Zafar.

To all my hometown GBC fam (Lew, Tom, AY, Larry, Dre, Gary, Kev aka DJ K Slay, McGee, Stash, yeah you, too, Saleeby and affiliates!), strong love forever and forever. And finally, to my parents, to my family near and allá, and to Andrea, for holding it down through thick and thin, through joy and sorrow. Love and more love.

ABOUT THE AUTHOR

AARON COLEMAN is a poet, translator, educator, and scholar of the African Diaspora. He is the recipient of fellowships from the National Endowment of the Arts, Cave Canem, the Fulbright Program, and the American Literary Translators Association. His debut poetry collection, *Threat Come Close*, was the winner of the Great Lakes Colleges Association New Writers Award, and his chapbook *St. Trigger*, won the Button Poetry Prize. He is also the translator of Afro-Cuban poet Nicolás Guillén's 1967 collection, *The Great Zoo,* selected for the Phoenix Poet Series by University of Chicago Press. His poems, essays, and translations have appeared in publications including *The New York Times*, *Boston Review*, *Callaloo*, and *Poetry* Magazine. From Metro-Detroit, Coleman has lived and worked with youth in locations including Spain, South Africa, Chicago, St. Louis, and Kalamazoo. He is an assistant professor of English and Comparative Literature in the Helen Zell Writers' Program at the University of Michigan.